Win
Like *Lin*

Noah Henley

Win
Like Lin

Finding Your Inner Linsanity on the Way to Breakout Success

SEAN DEVENEY

New York Chicago San Francisco Lisbon
London Madrid Mexico City
Milan New Delhi San Juan Seoul
Singapore Sydney Toronto

1 2 3 4 5 6 7 8 9 0   LSI/LSI 1 8 7 6 5 4 3 2

ISBN 978-0-07-180399-1
MHID 0-07-180399-8

e-ISBN 978-0-07-180335-9
e-MHID 0-07-180335-1

Sean Deveney is represented by Wheelhouse Literary Group, PO Box 110909, Nashville, TN 37222, www.WheelhouseLiteraryGroup.com.

McGraw-Hill books are available at special quantity discounts to use as premiums and sales promotions or for use in corporate training programs. To contact a representative, please e-mail us at bulksales@mcgraw-hill.com.

To my brother, Brian, and sister, Lisa, who have supported me through everything, and to my friends who always get me to the finish line.

CONTENTS

CONTENTS

ACKNOWLEDGMENTS

Special thanks to Phil Wagner and Will Wade for their insights, to Jim Barnett for his honesty, and to Eric Musselman and all the folks working to help players in the D League to keep their dreams alive.

Additional thanks to Landry Fields, Tyson Chandler, Kyle Lowry, Wesley Matthews, Raymond Ridder, Andre Iguodala, Steve Nash, Shawn Marion, and Dr. Jason Selk.

Win
Like Lin

THE
BEGINNING

"Where did this come from? . . . It feels like some
bizarro version of Rudy."

—*Ian Eagle, YES Network*

On February 4, 2012, with the Knicks trailing by 12 points early in the second quarter of a game against the lowly New Jersey Nets at Madison Square Garden, point guard Jeremy Lin took the ball over the halfcourt line and passed to teammate Toney Douglas. Lin accelerated along the sideline near Douglas, took a return pass, and broke to the basket. As he did, Douglas picked Lin's defender, allowing Lin to get to the rim as Nets center Jordan Williams came over to help defensively. Lin gave Williams a slight fake and laid the ball off the backboard and in. They were Lin's first two points of the night, and just his 36th points of the season.

But they were two points that would set off some of the most exhilarating, bizarre, and tumultuous weeks in the long history of the New York Knicks and the league in general, two points that altered the direction of the team, two points that would help inflame the enthusiasm of a city, two points that would mark the move of one player from fringe reserve journeyman to established NBA roster member finding his way in the league, that set off the amazing rise of an international star, and that would serve as a starting point in a cautionary tale about the vicissitudes of fame and big-time professional sports. The previous night, February 3, Knicks coach Mike D'Antoni—who was already, at that point, facing pressure to keep his job amid missed expectations and mounting disappointment—had juggled his playing rotation and inserted Lin into a loss to the Celtics in Boston, which dropped the Knicks to 8–15 on the season. Lin's appearance was unremarkable, as he finished with just two points in a little more than six minutes on the floor. It was a surprise that Lin got into the game so early, though, given that he had played so little all year, and afterward, D'Antoni explained that he was searching for a spark. "Just anything," he said. "Just trying to find some kind of rhyme or reason to things. Haven't quite found it yet."

Against the Nets, that spark was ignited. It was Lin, an unlikely source given that he had had just 38 games of experience at that point and had spent the previous six weeks buried deep on the Knicks bench. Lin finished the first half with six points. He scored seven more in the third quarter, matching his previous career high of 13 for a game. He took over in the fourth quarter, with 12 points, finishing with 25 on the night and leading the wayward Knicks to a much-needed win as the crowd chanted, "Jer-Em-Mee!" The scene was unbelievable, and fans and Knicks teammates cheered Lin on wildly. When Lin crashed through the defense and finished a difficult shot at the rim while drawing a foul in the second half of the game, Ian Eagle, veteran Nets broadcaster on the YES network, yelled, "Where did this come from?... It feels like some bizarro version of Rudy."

In the locker room afterward, Lin was having trouble processing his performance. Typically, reporters from local papers and broadcast media would crowd around the lockers of star players like Amar'e Stoudemire, Carmelo Anthony, and Tyson Chandler for postgame interviews. But now it was Lin, tucked into the far side of the Knicks locker room, who was crowded with microphones, something he'd experienced before but never because of an actual in-game performance. "It hasn't really sunk in yet," he said. "To be honest, I'm still kind of in shock about everything that happened. But I am just trying to soak it all in right now."

It started with two points, with a give-and-go play (one of the most basic plays in basketball) and a layup. There has been a lot to soak in since, both positive and negative. First up was Lin's desire to prove the Nets game was not a fluke. Two nights later, Lin scored 28 points to beat Utah, and followed that with 23 in a win over Washington. That led to a nationally televised game against Kobe Bryant and the Lakers, a team that figured to put Lin's little three-game run to the test. On the night before the game, Bryant was asked about Lin's recent play. Bryant said he didn't know anything about it.

He found out, firsthand. Lin notched 38 points against the Lakers for the Knicks' fourth straight win, and even before the game was over, Lin had become an instant icon in New York, across the NBA, and even in China and Taiwan, where he has family. That week, he was featured on the cover of *Sports Illustrated* and then again the following week, just the 10th athlete to appear on *SI*'s cover on consecutive weeks, joining the likes of Michael Jordan, Kareem Abdul-Jabbar, Steve Young, Mike Tyson, and Mark McGwire. His story went beyond the sports world. Just five games after that Saturday against the Nets, he was on the cover of *Time* magazine, with the headline, "LINSANITY!" There was a feeling that it was all happening too fast, that Lin still had a long way to go and a lot to prove as a player. But the league, and especially the disappointing Knicks, was in need of a hero, and Lin seemed an unlikely one worth celebrating—with a doubly rare background in the NBA as an Asian American Harvard graduate. Once the cork pops, of course, there is no putting the champagne back in the bottle.

Lin's story quickly became the stuff of legend and, almost as quickly, a tale of the slings and arrows that follow outrageous fortune in an era of accelerated media and micro-news cycles. The sequence of events before Lin's arrival on the international sports scene is a feel-good story that's almost too incredible to grasp. On the night before the Nets win, Lin revealed, he had slept on the couch of friend and teammate Landry Fields, because the couch he had been sleeping on—at his brother's apartment in Manhattan—was occupied by visiting friends. He did not yet have his own apartment because he had already been cut by the Warriors and the Rockets, and because his contract was not yet guaranteed, he knew there was the possibility that the Knicks would do the same. From there, he found himself at the epicenter of the sports world, gaining rave reviews courtesy of fans ranging from Hall of Famer Magic Johnson, to film director and Knicks fan Spike Lee, to actress Bo Derek, to Facebook founder Mark Zuckerberg, to President Obama. He was a hit on the social media scene. According to one study, Lin's name was tweeted more than 2.6 million times in one week, and his number of followers on Twitter doubled to more than 380,000 in a matter of four days. By the time he had led the Knicks over the Lakers, he had topped 500,000 Twitter followers.

At the time, one of Lin's newest teammates, guard J. R. Smith, was in China, finishing a stint on a pro contract there. Fans in China and Taiwan had latched onto Lin, too, to the point where Lin's family in Taiwan had left their homes, prompting Lin to make a public plea to Taiwanese media members to respect his family's privacy. Smith said that, on the other side of the globe, he was able to pick up on the effect Lin was having on the Knicks, and on fans. "I saw a lot of YouTube highlights and stuff like that," Smith said. "Just watching him play was crazy. He really inspires a lot of people around here, and around the world. He is definitely a person people can look up to. When you hear his story, it gives you hope for anything."

Hope for anything is, of course, a broad sentiment, and too often positive stories in the sports world are spun into recognizable clichés. The underdog story—the bizarro Rudy—is the most common, going back to David playing slingshots against Goliath, and the rise of Lin's star does fit the bill for that kind of narrative. But there is more to the Lin tale than platitudes, and the early focus on his newfound fame and success ignored the more important aspects of his story, almost like celebrating a lottery winner for his riches rather than someone who worked hard to earn the same. By the same token, the struggles of the Knicks that followed his whirlwind emergence, struggles that would eventually lead to D'Antoni's departure from the team, don't diminish what Lin did to make himself an NBA player in the past two years and beyond. Lin did not rise out of nowhere. The conventional wisdom that he was a hidden gem on the bench of three teams in the past year, that all he needed was for some forward-thinking coach to see that he belonged on the floor and that stardom would ensued is oversimplified.

Lost in the underdog narrative, and the Knicks' eventual overhaul, are the real lessons to be gleaned from the rise of Lin, the ones that can be taken from his acceptance of his unusual route to the NBA, the ones that can be taken from his off-season work, the ones that can be taken from his ability to remain prepared for opportunities and the necessity of coping with both sudden success and just as sudden adversity. Things can change, and they can change fast. It was only one week, after all, between the time D'Antoni put Lin into the Boston game out of desperation and the time Lin torched the Lakers and sealed his celebrity. It was only about a month after that, though, that D'Antoni was gone. What should matter to most of us is not the sudden fame and what will be sure to be an increase in fortune when Lin signs a new contract this summer. What should matter is what happened before the change, the work and preparation that Lin put in before that breakout game against the Nets, when virtually no NBA fans knew who he was and his career was hanging by a very tenuous thread. What should matter is how Lin handled himself and his teammates in those weeks in which he was the never-ending highlight on SportsCenter.

And what should matter, too, is what happens from here. Lin is only 23 years old, and he came into this season hoping merely to establish himself as a legitimate NBA player. He didn't expect or ask for stardom, nor did he expect the rigors that came once that stardom was thrust upon him. The so-called Linsanity has waned into daily routine, which can only help Lin because, though he handled the flood of attention with grace, it was entirely new to him and he never really seemed comfortable with it. Now that he has garnered this level of attention, things have changed. Opponents are figuring out how to defend him, players are gearing up to put forth their best effort against him, the Knicks have had trouble with chemistry, and the Knicks' replacing of D'Antoni with assistant Mike Woodson has changed the team's offensive system in a way that marginalizes what Lin does best. This is all new territory for Lin, but having shown what sorts of skills he can bring to an NBA team, he now needs to build on those skills, eliminate the flaws in his game, and confirm his place in the league.

But this story is only in the very early going, and improvement has always been part of the plan for Lin. Put aside the facile out-of-nowhere storyline, and you'll see that Lin actually worked very hard to get to the NBA, and will have to work just as hard to maintain the level of play he showed in his first few weeks as a starter. The magazine covers and cultural-icon status were a shock. No one had envisioned his strange path to stardom—at best, he seemed to be a player who could carve out a reasonably long career in pro basketball, with a degree from Harvard as a fallback. Now, he can shrug off the Linsanity distraction that came with his initial play in New York, because his goal was much more modest when the season began. "I always told myself, for this year, coming into this year, I wanted to establish myself in the rotation and not be the 12th to 15th guy on the team," Lin said. "Obviously, that's what I wanted to do, and that's what I felt like I could do. But the reality of the situation was that I was the 12th to 15th guy, and that's why I got waived a couple of times. I'm just thankful to God that I am here with New York."

He is striving to stay in New York now. As new obstacles present themselves, Lin is finding that he is, at least, what he had hoped he would be at this point in life all along: an established second-year NBA basketball player trying to improve his game and help his team win.

From the long and very unusual path Lin took to get there, there are plenty of lessons to be learned.

CHAPTER 1

EMBRACE THE ROAD LESS TRAVELED

"Everybody's overlooked him for the last 20 years, probably since grade school....To his credit, he just kept plugging away."

—Mike D'Antoni

March 9, 2011
CNN American Morning studio
Columbus Circle, New York, New York

Jeremy Lin, point guard for the Warriors, was seated in a metal chair across from anchor T. J. Holmes early on a Wednesday morning before Golden State's game against the Nets, taping a segment for CNN's weekend morning show. Six days earlier, when the team had had an off day in Boston, Lin had gone over to Cambridge to stop by the registrar's office at Harvard University, where he had earned a degree in economics, graduating the previous spring. Lin had not been able to get the diploma, though, because he had missed the ceremony to go through NBA predraft workouts. This is what Holmes wanted to discuss.

Holmes introduced the segment by saying, "Which of these names doesn't belong: LeBron James, Dwyane Wade, Jeremy Lin, Carmelo Anthony? You would probably say Jeremy Lin, but the name does belong. Everybody I named is a standout in the NBA. But Jeremy Lin is a standout for a different reason—because he is the only NBA player right now that also holds a Harvard degree."

Holmes cited three things that made Lin a standout: his Harvard education, his ethnicity, and his religious devotion. Lin, even at that point in his career, was getting accustomed to attention that came from his uniqueness as an NBA player. When he had signed with the Warriors as an undrafted free agent in September 2011, the team had held an informal media availability, and more reporters showed up than for any other Warriors preseason press conference in recent memory—a very unusual circumstance for an undrafted rookie. Lin averaged only 2.6 points per game as a rookie with the Warriors, but because of his background, he got as many media requests as anyone on the team, including star players Monta Ellis and Stephen Curry. Warriors public relations director Raymond Ridder estimates that the team turned down 80 percent of those requests, in an effort to limit the pressure on Lin.

Talking with Holmes, Lin was proud of his path—but, at the same time, the controlled media access was a good indicator that he and his agent, Roger Montgomery, didn't want attention to his backstory outpacing his actual on-court accomplishments. "I definitely stand out for sure, and I know my story is very unique," Lin told Holmes. "But that's something I embrace and enjoy. Just this whole journey has been a blessing from God. For me to be here, I am just taking it one day at a time and really enjoying it."

Saul Mariaschin started his collegiate basketball career at Syracuse, but left when he enlisted in the Navy to fight in World War II. When he came back, he enrolled at Harvard and was the captain of the Crimson basketball team for two years, leading them to their first NCAA tournament spot in 1946. After that,

Mariaschin played 43 games in 1947–48 for the Celtics of what was then called the Basketball Association of America, but, as the story has it, his father-in-law did not want him traveling so much, so he quit. After Mariaschin left, Ed Smith starred at Harvard until 1951, when he was chosen No. 6 in the NBA draft by the Knicks. Smith also went to war—he fought in Korea—and when he returned in 1953, he got started on his pro career in New York. But he injured his hand early on and never got a footing with the Knicks. He played just 11 games, scoring 28 points.

The 54 games played by Mariaschin and Smith had been the sum total of Harvard's American professional basketball output. There have been eight U.S. presidents and more than 50 Nobel Prize laureates to go through the halls of Harvard undergrad or graduate schools. But before Lin, there were just 54 games' worth of basketball.

Wat Misaka was a 5-7 point guard from Ogden, Utah, who helped lead the University of Utah to championships in the NIT and NCAA tournaments in the '40s, and went from there to become the first Asian American player in pro basketball history—he logged three games and seven points for the Knicks in the 1947–48 season. Since then, Asian Americans like Raymond Townsend (who is half Filipino) and Rex Walters (half Japanese) have played in the league, as have Asian imports like Yao Ming and Yi Jianlian. But in the NBA, Asian American players have been very rare.

Even before NBA teams sized up Lin when he was coming out of college during the predraft period in 2010, he had perception working against him. Typically, NBA players come from college powerhouses like North Carolina or Kansas or Connecticut. They don't come from Ivy League schools, and certainly not from

Harvard. They're also not typically of Asian descent. In fact, players at the collegiate level are rarely Asian American. NCAA figures for Lin's senior year showed that of the 5,182 male basketball players in Div. I, just 26 were Asian American. One of those 26 was Lin, the son of Taiwanese immigrants.

When Lin went undrafted after completing college, his Harvard coach, former Duke star Tommy Amaker, wondered whether it was embedded, preconceived notions about whether an Asian American from Harvard had a place in the NBA that had kept him shut out of the draft. There may be something to that theory—scouts very often use comparisons as one part of evaluating players, and there just aren't many players who immediately look like Lin. Indeed, Lin, too, wonders if Amaker is right, especially when he still hears compliments about his game couched in adverbs like *deceptively* or *surprisingly*.

"I think it has something to do with it," Lin said at this year's All-Star game. "I don't know how much. But I think just being Asian American, obviously when you look at me, I'm going to have to prove myself more so again and again and again, and some people may not believe it. I know a lot of people say I'm deceptively athletic and deceptively quick, and I'm not sure what's deceptive. But it could be the fact I'm Asian American. But I think that's fine. It's something that I embrace, and it gives me a chip on my shoulder. But I'm very proud to be Asian American, and I love it."

The more Lin can establish himself in the NBA, the more he can change the assumptions made about Asian Americans and sports in this country. That's something Miami Heat coach Erik Spoelstra, a Filipino American who has a strong following in the Philippines, can understand. "It's a great story," Spoelstra said before the Heat faced the Knicks for the first time. "There's no doubt about it, the fact that he came from oblivion really from the standpoint of, he was cut, had to go to the NBDL multiple times, it shows his fortitude, his character, his resiliency. I don't know him, but I would guess he has a similar perspective as me about it. It is terrific to be involved with changing people's perceptions, and the world is changing. But, ultimately, and hopefully years from now, the story will be about the basketball story. It won't be about ethnicity."

To be fair to NBA teams, there was more to teams overlooking Lin on draft night than ethnicity. There was also a pretty universal scouting report when he was coming out of Harvard, even after he averaged 17.1 points in his junior and senior years, finishing as league MVP: Lin had talent, and there were some who felt he could develop, but he was very thin and, though he had improved his accuracy, he had an awkward, over-the-head shooting style that would be easier to defend in the NBA than it had been in the Ivy League. There are two rounds in the draft, with 60 total picks, and, generally, no one would accuse league executives of being closed-minded when it comes to finding players—there were players from 10 foreign countries chosen in Lin's draft. When teams looked at Lin, perhaps some saw an Asian American and had no point of reference. But teams also just didn't see unique NBA potential.

It wasn't as though his entry into the NBA was the first instance in which Lin had been misjudged. In fact, it was the same for Lin coming out of high school. In 2005, when Lin was a junior at Palo Alto High in California, he sent out tapes and a résumé, targeting teams he thought were a match scholarship-wise. These were mostly mid-major schools, not the kind of colleges that typically send top-seeded teams to NCAA tournaments. But Lin got no real responses. He also tested out the Ivy League, which does not award athletic scholarships, and there was some interest, especially from Harvard and Brown. He considered taking a walk-on spot (without a scholarship, but with the chance to earn one through performance) at Pac-10 schools like UCLA, Cal, or Stanford—whose athletic department sits directly across the El Camino Real road from Lin's high school—but those were long shots. Stanford coach Trent Johnson offered Lin a chance at a walk-on spot, but when Johnson added two players (including current Knicks teammate and close friend Landry Fields) to an already packed recruiting class that had eventual NBA first-round picks Brook and Robin Lopez as well as Da'Veed Dildy, a point guard from Chicago, it was clear to Lin that there wasn't much room for him, even as a walk-on who simply had to walk across the street.

In the summer of his junior year, when Lin participated in the series of major Amateur Athletic Union tournaments held annually in Las Vegas—tournaments that are a mecca for college coaches seeking players—he wasn't attracting much attention. After one game, his high school coach, Peter Diepenbrock, approached Harvard assistant Bill Holden, asking for his opinion on his point guard. Holden told Diepenbrock that Lin should consider Div. III schools. But Holden watched Lin again a few weeks later, in a more competitive game at another AAU tournament. Facing tougher competition, Lin's intensity stood out. Holden's opinion of Lin changed. Now he thought Lin should be Harvard's top priority. Eventually, coach Frank Sullivan went to Palo Alto to meet Lin's parents and offer him a spot on his team.

Such commitments are nonbinding, though, and over the following season, Harvard coaches watched anxiously as Lin and Palo Alto rolled through an impressive 32-1 season, not an easy thing to do for a public school playing Div. II basketball in the state of California. But the Vikings downed top-tier schools, including Archbishop Mitty of San Jose twice in a span of eight days, and earned the right to play for the state championship in March 2006, at Arco Arena, home of the NBA's Sacramento Kings. The opponent: nationally ranked powerhouse Mater Dei of Santa Ana.

Palo Alto won, 51-47, an unforgettable upset. Mater Dei featured a frontcourt with a 7-foot center and two forwards who were 6-foot-8, while the Vikings did not have a player over 6-foot-6—Paly's Kheaton Scott, just 6-foot-1, jumped for the opening tipoff. (Scott, fittingly, won the tip.) But the key play in the game was a shot from beyond even the NBA 3-point line with the shot clock running down, 2:07 to play and Palo Alto up by only two points, a shot that banked in. That was, of course, a shot by Lin, who led his team with 17 points. "The bank shot broke our back," Mater Dei coach Gary McKnight told the *Los Angeles Times*.

Lin finished his senior year at Palo Alto with averages of 15.1 points, 7.1 assists, 6.2 rebounds, and 4.8 steals. He was an All-State selection and was one of seven finalists for California's Mr. Basketball that year, with fellow NBAers like Ryan Anderson, James Harden, and Chase Budinger. Lin also was named player of the year by the *San Francisco Chronicle*, as well as the *San Jose Mercury-News*.

As for his college choices, not much changed. Stanford and UCLA were interested in Lin as a walk-on. Sullivan and his assistants were worried that another Div. I program would come to Lin with a scholarship. Didn't happen.

If Lin had been overlooked by the NBA before getting his chance with the Knicks, then, it's nothing new. "Everbody's over-looked him for the last 20 years, probably since grade school," then-Knicks head coach Mike D'Antoni said. "To his credit, he just kept plugging away. He's got an opportunity, and he is making the most of it. I am sure along the way, people have kind of liked him because he did get picked up on waivers twice. A lot of guys don't get picked up on waivers, so somebody obviously saw something, but it wasn't enough to get him over the hump."

———————— ▬▬▬▬▬ ————————

Here, though, is a spot at which the simple narrative of Lin as an underappreciated sports underdog should be resisted—his path to NBA stardom is more complicated than that. Lin's rise has been unusual, and his story is far from complete. But he's not the only undrafted player to make it in the NBA, and there are plenty of pro athletes whose road to success takes bizarre detours.

"ESPN will bludgeon you with Jeremy Lin and his 'struggle,'" said former Knicks coach and ESPN analyst Jeff Van Gundy. "That's the other thing that drives me crazy about the media—what do you mean, struggle? Struggle compared to who? Minor league baseball players who spend 10 years in the minors just to get one at-bat in the big leagues? This idea that he struggled—he was in the NBA last year. Just because he did not get to play right away does not mean anything, a lot of guys don't get to play right away. Sometimes I think we're missing what a great story it is because we're trying to make it a different story. This guy, it doesn't matter where he went to college. It doesn't matter what his religion is. It doesn't matter that he went to the D League twice. What matters is that this guy can play."

Yes, what matters is that this guy can play. It has been an uncommon journey for Lin, but in the end, that is irrelevant—he kept his focus on what he could control, he did not shrug his shoulders and walk away when told he should go to a Div. III college, he did not cave to the stereotypes around his school or his ethnicity, he did not let go of his goal when the '10 draft ended and he was without a team. Lin's ability may have been missed by scouts and analysts of all stripes, but the annals of the NBA, and professional sports in general, are littered with stories of players who were not correctly evaluated—positively or negatively. There are plenty of players whose career arcs go in the opposite direction from Lin's, stories in which can't-miss prospects do miss, and by wide margins.

One of the great coincidences of the Warriors' decision to release Lin is that they did so in order to clear room to sign center DeAndre Jordan—an underappreciated talent himself, who fell into the draft's second round in 2008. When the Clippers matched Golden State's offer to Jordan, the Warriors instead signed free agent Kwame Brown to take the spot Jordan would have held. Brown was, back in 2001, the first player chosen in the NBA draft, by the Washington Wizards. At the time, the Wizards were being run by the greatest player in league history, Michael Jordan. But Jordan missed, badly, on Brown, who has had an unremarkable career playing for six different teams, averaging more than 10 points per game only once in his career. After signing with the Warriors, Brown tore a pectoral muscle and missed most of the season.

Brown's path is as notable in a negative direction as Lin's path is notable in a positive one. "To me, what Jeremy Lin shows is that outliers are always going to happen; no matter how good your predictive models are or whatever, there are always going to be players who are going to defy or exceed it," said ESPN's John Hollinger, a stats guru speaking at the Sloan Sports Analytics Conference. "You can't always map improvement from a player, it is not always in increments. Sometimes, guys shoot up or shoot down, and it is very difficult to model for that."

There are players who have had excellent NBA careers even after being ignored in the draft, guys who were too difficult to model—players like the former Knick John Starks, the Pistons' Ben Wallace, and the Timberwolves' Brad Miller, who all went on to earn All-Star spots, as well as forward Bruce Bowen, whose defensive toughness helped the San Antonio Spurs to three championships. Bowen's contribution was so appreciated in San Antonio that the team retired his jersey this year.

Guard Wesley Matthews also went undrafted in 2009, despite averaging 18.3 points for a nationally ranked Marquette team. But he was given a chance with the Jazz and, after proving that he belonged in the NBA with an outstanding rookie year in which he averaged 9.4 points and moved into the starting lineup, was awarded a five-year, $34 million contract from the Trailblazers and averaged 15.9 points in his second season. Matthews uses his status as an undrafted players as motivation, as part of who he is professionally.

"I am always going to get better, because I am always going to work," Matthews said. "That's what going undrafted teaches you. There's a whole bunch of different paths to get here, and for me, it was the undrafted route. Some guys are going [to] get drafted in the first round, some are going in the second round, some have to go overseas and then come back. But you have to be level-headed; you can't let yourself [get] too high or too low. I am a stronger person for going through that process. As long as you work and as long as you believe, you can make it here. I embrace that."

That's been a key for Lin, too. Every player in the league has a backstory. Lin doesn't shrug off the uniqueness of his own story. He knows the fact that he went undrafted or that he is Asian American or that he went to Harvard or that he is religious, all of it doesn't matter. He embraces it, and stays confident that he can play. "There's been times when there's discouragement, you know, bad game and it's like, hmm, how good can I be?" Lin said. "Can I play at this level? Whether it's in college or the pre-draft process or early in my rookie year. But it's frustrating anytime you don't play because as athletes we all have pride."

CHAPTER 2

DON'T SHORTCHANGE YOUR TALENT

"Jeremy came to us with all the attributes that you're seeing now—his ability to get to the rim, his toughness. . . . He had all of that, we didn't develop any of that, that's in his DNA."

—*Eric Musselman, Reno Bighorns*
(NBA Development League)

November 19, 2011
Lavietes Pavilion
Boston, Massachusetts

Though he had played four seasons at Harvard in this building right across the Charles River from Cambridge, it would have been easy for the crowd of 2,200, which included Boston mayor Tom Menino, to overlook Jeremy Lin's presence. Sure, he was the one with a jersey hanging up in the conference room above the court, arguably the best home player the building had seen. But now, Lin was in town for a charity game hosted by Celtics All-Star point guard Rajon Rondo. Another Boston All-Star, Paul Pierce, was also at Lavietes Pavilion, as well as NBA notables like Atlanta's Josh Smith, Memphis's Rudy Gay, and Oklahoma City's Kendrick Perkins. Lin had been invited, too, but in the pecking order of players taking part in the game, he was decidedly on the lower tier, despite his Harvard history.

The NBA was, at the time, in the fifth month of a grinding lockout, with the league's owners and players association unable to bridge their differences in settling on a new collective bargaining agreement. That would change when the sides had a breakthrough a week later, but at the time, that opening seemed distant, if not impossible. The chances of playing a 2011–12 season looked slim. Summer league, training camp, and the first month and a half of the season had been canceled already. Players had been flocking overseas for much of the off-season, especially fringe players who had not been making sizable NBA paychecks. Lin was considering an offer from Teramo Basket in Italy, as well as other international possibilities, and was prepared to return to California, get his visa and passport in order, and go overseas to play.

Even then, it didn't take much to notice that Lin looked somewhat different from what he had in his limited time with the Warriors. He was bigger and stronger in the shoulders and legs, and though the charity game itself was far more show than competition, he looked like a better shooter—in one stretch of the third quarter, he made five 3-pointers, which is as many as he had attempted over the entire course of his rookie season the previous year in Golden State (he had made just one of those attempts). Still, the lockout was wearing on him, as it was on most NBA players.

"It's just different because I have never had such a long period where I could not play organized basketball," Lin said after the game. "I am new to it, and a lot of the guys are, too. It's been frustrating, but we just try to make sure everybody's working out, so we just kind of contact each other and stay in touch."

Perhaps Lin did not know it at the time, but the NBA's lockout was probably a turning point for his transformation from fringe benchwarmer in Golden State to sudden star in New York. If there had been no lockout, Lin would most likely have been asked by the Warriors to spend about two weeks in Las Vegas in July playing summer league basketball, with rookies and fellow young players. He probably would have done some sort of charity tour, either through the NBA or through the Warriors. He would have reported to Oakland in September to begin workouts with his teammates, and he would have jumped right into training camp and preseason games in October. In a normal off-season, he would not have had more than six or seven consecutive weeks to work out and get ready.

He was right when he said that he had never gone so long in his life without playing organized basketball, but it may well be that he needed that break to work on the two major flaws in his game: his shooting and his lack of strength. When it began, he didn't know that the lockout would afford him seven uninterrupted months of training time, not the usual paltry six or seven weeks. But he did know that if he was going to have to cope with forced time off while the owners and the union fought over a new contract, he was going to use every day he could to get better.

That was the idea when Lin showed up at the Sparta Performance Science facility in Menlo Park, California, after recovering from a minor knee surgery that spring. There, he met with Dr. Phil Wagner, a physician who specializes in physiology and was the strength and conditioning coach at both Cal and UCLA. "The lockout was actually a huge, huge blessing for Jeremy, because he was able to work with us for four straight months," Wagner said. "That is an eternity for an athlete in the off-season, when you are lucky to have two or two and a half months. It was a big advantage for him because he needed to just focus on himself physically and not necessarily on being on the court playing five-on-five games. It is hard to get athletes to look at things that way, but he had no choice. He took full advantage of that time."

Wagner takes an advanced, science-based approach to athlete training, and the first thing he had Lin do was test his leap on a "force plate," which Wagner describes as a "$20,000 bathroom scale built into the ground." The plate would measure the amount of force that Lin created on different planes when he leapt, and from that, Wagner could use special software to map a "fingerprint" of Lin's entire nervous system. What Wagner found as a baseline for Lin was that he was too loose—for an athlete to maximize his quickness, agility, and jumping, he needs to strike the ideal balance between muscle mass and flexibility, tightness and looseness. This is known as a stretch-shortening cycle.

"Think of it like you would think of a rubber band that you can stretch and snap back," Wagner said. "In order to generate force, you need to generate tension, and to do that, you can't be too loose—you need the rubber band to snap back. So for Jeremy, we needed to make his cycle tighter, we needed to add tension, and we did that by doing a lot of heavy-weight, short-repetition exercises. Squatting, pressing, lunges, all the things that would work to improve his muscle mass. He needed it. It was a difficult program for anyone, but he was determined. He was as focused as any athlete we have had."

While Lin was working on his build with Wagner, he was also working on his shooting with a well-known Northern California coach, Doc Scheppler, whose Pinewood High girls teams have won five California state championships. Scheppler had coached Lin's high school coach, Peter Diepenbrock, and Lin had hoped to begin working out with him the previous summer. But, again, typical summers for players can get clouded with other commitments, and Lin was busy—first, he took part in the NBA's summer league with Dallas in order to try to secure a contract, and, once he did, traveled to Taiwan with his parents (his first visit to their native country since he was 14) to play in a charity game hosted by Chinese star center Yao Ming. Not a bad decision. Lin was already a celebrity in Taiwan, and even met Taiwan's president, Ma Ying-jeou, a graduate of Harvard Law School.

But the summer of 2011 was different. The lockout afforded Lin plenty of time for shot work. Perfecting a jump shot requires long hours, but it also requires a thorough understanding of what a player is doing wrong and why. Too often, players approach shooting practice as a matter of repetition, thinking that slinging up hundreds of shots daily will provide a fix for faulty technique. Too often, though, repetition just leads to reinforcing the small, almost imperceptible bad habits that can knock shooters awry. What might look like minor details to most—hand placement, stance width, wrist action, release point, jump timing—add up as a shooter goes through his motion. Those details are vital in establishing a consistent and ideal shooting style, and slight problems with any step along the way can lead to erratic shooting. Though he had improved since his days as a sophomore at Harvard, and had come a very long way since his awkward shot at Palo Alto, Lin still had slight problems at virtually every spot in his shooting motion.

"You could see it in warm-ups when he was a rookie," said Warriors broadcaster Jim Barnett, an 11-year NBA veteran. "He is a great guy and someone you want to root for, but I would watch him and he would do the drill where you go and shoot from different spots on the floor, you go around the perimeter.

I never saw him make more than three in a row. He had trouble being consistent with the shot, especially left and right, and that usually means something is wrong with your motion, with your feet, something. You could tell he pulled his hands too far back over his head when he shot, which means you're not shooting quick enough. And I remember thinking, if he doesn't change his shooting style, he is going to have a hard time staying in the NBA. He could do a lot of things well, but he just needed to get that shot down right."

Lin did change his style. In fact, he overhauled it. Even while he was recovering from his surgery, Lin got started with Scheppler, working on how and where he released, loosening his grip on the ball, and developing a more consistent wrist snap. Lin widened his stance so that his feet were more directly beneath his shoulders, and changed his rhythm to keep his jump more in control. He worked on what Barnett saw as his biggest flaw, pulling the shot too far back over his head. He practiced running jumpers from short and medium distance, a staple for point guards facing shot-blocking centers. There were so many little things to work out, and Lin would visit Scheppler a few times a week, then take the lessons back to the practice court. "I know my [shooting] percentage is low," Lin said. "But I got a shooting coach this summer and he helped me a ton with my shot. So I am not going to stop shooting if I think it is a good shot. I understand my percentage is low, and that's obviously a criticism people are going to have of me."

When he showed up at his old home floor in Boston in November, though, Lin had not played in a real game since April 13, more than seven months. He had spent the summer changing his body and his shot, but without any time on the court in competitive situations against other NBA players, there was no way to tell whether all these changes would matter at all.

———————————————

Those who had worked with Lin at different stages in his life are not surprised by the way he approached the lockout and used the time away from the game to address his weaknesses. That has been a hallmark of Lin's development throughout his basketball life: the willingness to steer criticism into opportunities for positive development, to turn frustration into improvement. *New York Times* writer Howard Beck recounted a story from Scheppler in which Lin was playing a shooting game called "Beat the Ghost." Lin lost, 21-17, and kicked the ball afterward. Before he began to go through the predraft process in 2010, Lin got the help of shooting coach David Jones, to whom Lin paid daily visits. Even at Harvard, assistant coach Will Wade, now at Virginia Commonwealth, said that Lin showed a characteristic of many great athletes—no matter how many positive things he might have done over the course of a game, he had a hard time letting go of the negative.

"There were games where he would go out and play great," Wade said. "He would have 20 or so points, he would shoot the ball well, he would make the right passes, we would win the game. But he'd miss two free throws. You'd talk to him after the game and you could just see the look on his face; his mind was on those free throws, he was upset with himself. And the next morning, you'd go into the gym and he'd be practicing free throws. That's the kind of player who always wants to get better. That's the kind of player Jeremy was."

Lin has a certain amount of God-given ability. Anyone in the NBA or any professional sport— or any profession at all for that matter—has some ability. But not everyone is willing to do what is required to get the most out of that ability, and too often natural gifts go untapped, even among professional athletes with millions of dollars in contracts at stake. The last NBA draft as of this writing was held in June 2011—go back five years before that, to the '06 draft, and already 14 of the 30 players chosen with first-round picks are out of the NBA or never played in the league at all. When there is discussion of the many times Lin has been snubbed, then, it should be put into the wider context of the vagaries of talent evaluation. Players who are tall, athletic, and gifted are easy to spot, and those are the ones that college recruiters will pursue hotly. They're also the ones who will capture the imagination of those running the draft for NBA teams. But there's no way to evaluate determination and willingness to improve. There's no way to tell which players will shortchange their talent and which will maximize it.

And it's more than just a willingness to get better through practice. Again, maximizing talent is not just about hard work and time spent—it requires an understanding of what needs to be fixed and how to go about doing so. That's what Wade saw in Lin with his frustration over missed free throws, what Scheppler found with his perimeter shooting, what Wagner found with his workouts. Throughout his career, Lin has focused not on practicing the things he is already good at, but on working through his weaknesses.

"I think a lot of that attitude goes back to Tommy Amaker," Wade said. "He and Jeremy had a really special relationship. Jeremy's sophomore year, that was the first time he had really played important minutes, and it was obvious he was struggling with how to handle it. Tommy challenged him to get better as a leader and as a player. Tommy knew how good he could be and wanted to make sure Jeremy understood that, too. He had a way of boosting his confidence and at the same time always making sure he knew he would have to get better to be as good a player as he could be. He thought Jeremy was an NBA player all along."

Amaker took over at Harvard for Frank Sullivan when Lin was a sophomore. Lin had averaged 12.6 points that year and shot an abysmal 27.9 percent from the 3-point line in his first year with Amaker. But he took Amaker's challenge to heart, worked with assistant coach Kenny Blakeney every morning on improving his range, and was a transformed player as a junior, averaging 17.8 points and a sterling 40.0 percent on 3-pointers. Lin remains close with Blakeney even now.

Eric Musselman, who had two tours as an NBA head coach, now coaches in the NBA's Developmental League and coached Lin when he was a rookie and was sent to play at Reno by the Warriors. Lin averaged 18.0 points and shot 47.7 percent from the field (38.9 percent from the 3-point line) with Reno, but he still was focused on the things he was not doing well. "Jeremy came to us with all the attributes that you're seeing now—his ability to get to the rim, his toughness, he's a great hustle player, dives after loose balls," Musselman said. "He had all of that, we didn't develop any of that, that's in his DNA. But he wanted to become a better pick-and-roll player, and I think we helped him with that. Mostly because he wanted to learn, he wanted to break down how he could get better with it. He is a very smart player, and he approached things that way. He wanted to gain confidence in his 3-point shot, too, and I think he is getting better and better with that."

Again, it is not just the volume of work, it is the quality of the work. Honing athletic skill requires the engagement not just of one's body, but of one's brain as well. When Lin was trying to bulk up at Sparta, he did not simply check in and do the exercises as he was told to do them. He was ripe with questions, a desire to understand how the work he was doing would bring in results that would help him on the court. "He is one of the best students we have had here," Wagner said. "He is obviously an intelligent guy, and that works for us because all of what we do is very science-oriented. He was not just coming in and taking orders. He had to have an understanding in order to make the workout more effective for him. For Jeremy it was always, 'Why am I doing this? How is it going to help me? What are the reasons?' That is something we want; we want to be able to show them the science behind it and have them understand that. That makes it a lot easier to teach them."

By the time Lin showed up for the charity exhibition in Boston, he had already changed. He had added 15 points of muscle, Wagner said, and lost three pounds of fat. He had improved his vertical leap by 3½ inches. His quickness measurement had improved by a whopping 32 percent. "All of that makes him better on the court," Wagner said. "When you watch him now, you can see how it benefits him. When he drives into the paint, he is bigger and stronger and is much better able to take contact and still get a shot off."

Lin's inherent talent never caused the eyes of college recruiters to widen, never caused NBA scouts looking for off-the-charts leaping and quickness. But Lin has shown the willingness to work to sharpen the talent that he does have.

CHAPTER 3

SEIZE
OPPORTUNITY

"Great kid and he's a hell of a player. . . . It
makes you wonder how many guys are out there
who have just slipped through the cracks and
didn't find the right circumstances."

—*Steve Kerr*

January 7, 2009
Conte Forum
Chestnut Hill, Massachusetts

For Boston College, this game was expected to be a speed bump. The Eagles were ranked No. 17 in the nation, had won 10 straight games, and, three days earlier, had gone to Chapel Hill and knocked off the top-ranked team in basketball, North Carolina. The 3,174 fans boosting the home team were raucous, and the opponent was merely Harvard, which had never beaten a ranked opponent in school history and hadn't beaten the Eagles in more than 10 years. Boston College was a 17.5-point favorite.

Then the game started. BC got off to a 17-11 lead, but Harvard fought back with a 10-0 run. The Crimson led, 33-27 at the half, and it was junior Jeremy Lin who set the tone for the second half by stripping the ball from All-Atlantic Coast Conference guard Tyrese Rice and converting a breakaway layup. Lin made a 3-pointer from the corner to put Harvard up by 11 points, and from there, coach Tommy Amaker leaned heavily on Lin to close the game, calling repeated isolation plays in which Harvard would clear out space for Lin and allow him to decide whether to score himself or feed a teammate with a pass.

Harvard won, 82-70, a watershed moment for the program. Lin finished with 27 points on 11-for-16 shooting. He had eight assists and six steals in the game, two coming at the expense of Rice. The win gave Harvard basketball national notoriety, important for a team that had not made an NCAA tournament appearance since 1946. "We hope that we can look back on this and see this as one of those defining moments," Amaker told Bloomberg after the win. "That story will be told much later down the road, but it would be nice if that were able to take place."

It did take place, during the 2011–12 season, as Harvard was nationally ranked for much of the year and made its first NCAA tournament appearance in 56 years. The win over BC three years earlier was a defining moment, helping Harvard build credibility nationally. Cynics could point out that Harvard won that game mostly because Boston College was still riding the adrenaline of the North Carolina win, that the Eagles were caught off guard, and that if the two teams had played 10 times, Harvard might have lost 9 of them. There is truth to that. But catching Boston College with its guard down meant a meaningful opportunity for Harvard, and the Crimson deserve credit—they did not squander it.

That was thanks in large part to the confidence that Amaker showed in Lin, the way he put the ball in Lin's hands and asked him to win the game for his team. This is a familiar refrain throughout Lin's career, whether it is the Div. II state championship upset over Mater Dei, his performance in front of members of the Harvard coaching staff at an AAU tournament, or future memorable moments that would crop up in the NBA—

when presented with a big stage, when given a chance to prove himself against tough competition, that's when Lin has shined. The BC game was an opportunity, and Lin grabbed it.

"It was one 'iso' after the other for Jeremy," former Harvard assistant coach Will Wade said. "Tommy wanted to put the ball in Jeremy's hands and have him win the game for us. Looking back, that was the game that changed everything for Jeremy. He was a lot more confident after that, his confidence in what he could do shot up. We had a lot of kids play great in that game, but Jeremy sort of set things up for everyone. Tommy gave him the opportunity to do something unforgettable on the biggest stage he'd ever been on. And he did it."

He would nearly do so again the following year, as a senior, when he led the Crimson into Connecticut to face 14th-ranked UConn. Going head-to-head with Huskies star Kemba Walker, Lin shot 11-for-18, scoring 30 points with nine rebounds and three steals. Walker had 20 points, and the Huskies held on for a 79-73 win, but Lin had again left his mark against a top-tier program. "He's a terrific basketball player," Connecticut coach Jim Calhoun said after that game. "What I really like about him is he's athletic, more than you think so. He controls his temperament to a really nice tempo. He knows how to play. He's one of the better kids, including Big East guards, who have come in here in quite some time."

Too often, stories told of Lin's career focus on those who mis-evaluated his talents and the biases that may have gone into those faulty evaluations, whether it was size, ethnicity, religion, or collegiate background. As we've already seen, that's an incomplete story, because it does not take into account the reality that Lin's game did need work, and it doesn't factor in the utterly immeasurable—Lin's willingness to put in that work to improve his game, and how much better he got after making those improvements. As important as those evaluations and snubs, though, are those who recognized what Lin could do and those who gave him a chance, people like Peter Diepenbrock, Bill Holden, Frank Sullivan, and Amaker. What matters even more is what Lin did when given an opportunity.

Skip ahead to the summer of 2010. Lin was not chosen on draft night, but he wasn't entirely forgotten. Dallas Mavericks general manager Donnie Nelson called Lin on the night of the draft and told him he had watched him during the predraft period and wanted him to play for Dallas's summer league team in Las Vegas. Nelson knew that one reason Lin had been overlooked was that he had been a shooting guard at Harvard, not a point guard, and scouts were not sure that Lin could make the transition to point guard in the NBA, a transition that had been the demise of many past college stars. But Nelson had had his eye on Lin throughout his Harvard career, and had seen enough of Lin to make him think that, with a little work, he could be a good NBA point guard—in fact, during his conversation with Lin, Nelson likened him to former Mavs star point guard Steve Nash, a two-time MVP and a likely Hall-of-Famer.

The Mavericks had hoped that Nelson's assessment of Lin would prove accurate, and that they could sign him after his summer league stint was over. The plan was to have Lin play the bulk of the year for the Texas Legends of the D League, adjusting to his new position under the watchful eye of Mavericks coaches—the Legends are based in Frisco, Texas, about 30 miles north of Dallas. But as an undrafted free agent, Lin went to Las Vegas without a contract, meaning that he was not playing strictly for the Mavericks, but for all 30 teams. Summer League was an opportunity to show those teams what they'd missed.

Lin was outstanding. The high point came in a matchup against Washington, which was supposed to feature Dallas first-rounder Roddy Beaubois against the No. 1 overall pick in the draft, point guard John Wall. Instead, down the stretch, it was Lin who was on the floor against Wall, decisively outplaying him in the fourth quarter—and riling up the Cox Pavilion crowd with his defense and hustle, his array of nifty drives to the basket, and his acrobatic layups. Lin finished with 13 points, six assists, four rebounds, and two steals. Former NBA star Chris Webber, the analyst for that game, said, "He's made a great impression.... What's really impressed me the most, I know he can shoot, but he has been attacking the basket and taking it amongst the trees, and I really like seeing that. You can tell he is athletic, and he has a little bit of swagger, and I love seeing that."

Wall still recalls that game. "You could tell he was going to be good," Wall said. "He could penetrate, he had a good first step, he knew how to score. I don't know why no one drafted him."

For Dallas's purposes, Lin played too well in summer league. When it was over, multiple teams were vying to sign Lin, and because he was a free agent, Dallas had no real leverage when it came to a contract. One of the teams seeking to sign Lin was Golden State, Lin's hometown team, and the Warriors offered a partially guaranteed two-year deal, an unusual step for an undrafted rookie. Some in the media questioned the move as pandering to the Bay Area's large Asian American population, and team owner Joe Lacob (who had bought the team with co-owner Peter Guber just a week earlier) admitted that Lin's ethnicity was a tangential benefit. But Lacob's son, Kirk, had also played against Lin in high school, and Lacob knew that Lin had talent and heart. And the Warriors had competition—in addition to the Mavericks, a handful of other teams were interested, including the Los Angeles Lakers. Golden State had to move decisively on Lin.

Lin took advantage of his opportunity to earn entry into the NBA with the Warriors. As a rookie with the Warriors, though, he did not get a chance to show what he could do. Golden State had two star players, Monta Ellis and Stephen Curry, at the two guard spots, and veteran Acie Law took the playing time behind them. When the Warriors cut him, Lin signed with the Rockets. Houston wanted to keep him, but the Rockets also needed a center, and waived Lin to create a roster spot for free agent Samuel Dalembert. Lin signed with the Knicks two days later, still not having had a chance to play significant NBA minutes. But within 40 days, that changed.

Houston Rockets point guard Kyle Lowry and Lin were not teammates for long, but there is a kinship between the two. Lowry came into the league undervalued—he was a first-round pick, but he slipped all the way to No. 26 in the draft and he spent his first two years in the league, playing limited minutes as a backup to Mike Conley, a Top-10 pick, in Memphis. Lowry was traded to Houston, where he was still a backup for a year and a half, before starter Aaron Brooks (who had won the league's Most Improved award in 2010) was injured. Thrust into the starting five last year, Lowry shined. He averaged 19.8 points and 8.1 assists in the month of March, after Brooks was traded. During the 2011–12 season he was nearly an All-Star. Lowry's emergence is less of a surprise than Lin's—he was a star at Villanova, after all, and a first-round pick—but he sees the parallels.

"He was the third guard here," Lowry said. "He was the third guard in New York. But the opportunity came, and he took full advantage of it. That's what matters. You can't get upset when you're not getting the opportunity; you just have to keep preparing and acting like it is going to come. Because you don't want to cheat yourself when that chance happens. He's a good player. I don't think anyone knew he would do it to that extent, but obviously he had some skill. If you can get an opportunity, like I did here, you have to take full advantage of it. He has done that, and he has done an unbelievable job with it. It is a story that you have just got to say 'wow' to, to appreciate the fact that he never gave up and he kept working hard."

The history of sports is full of stories of players who get sudden opportunities and thrive, dating back to the legend of Yankees first baseman Wally Pipp sitting out with a headache in 1925, giving Lou Gehrig a chance to take over at first base, where he played for 2,130 consecutive games (a legend that is only partially true). In the NFL, Rams backup quarterback Kurt Warner, a veteran of the Arena League, took over when starter Trent Green injured his knee, and led St. Louis to the 2000 Super Bowl. Two years later, Patriots star quarterback Drew Bledsoe got injured and gave way to little-known sixth-round draft pick Tom Brady, who went on to become one of the greatest quarterbacks in league history.

Lin is not likely heading to the Hall of Fame like those players, but there's no question he got what he could out of his brief window of opportunity. When he arrived in New York at the end of December, Lin was behind Toney Douglas and Mike Bibby on the point-guard depth chart, and would have been even lower had rookie Iman Shumpert been healthy and had free-agent signee Baron Davis not been recovering from a serious back issue. But Shumpert and Douglas are not ideal point guards—they're examples of shooting guards who probably can't make the transition to point guard—and Bibby is well past his prime. For Lin, opportunity was in New York. It just didn't seem that way, not at first.

On January 27, the Knicks were in Miami, and Lin had played just six games for New York, totaling about 22 minutes. NBA teams make a chaplain available to players before each game, and Lin joined several players in the chapel at American Airlines Arena. When the chaplain asked if there were any special prayer requests, Lin raised his hand—his contract would become guaranteed for the year on February 10, and Lin knew that with Baron Davis returning and rumors that the Knicks might sign veteran guard Mike James, he could very well be waived again. "I knew February 10th was right around the corner, so that was what was on my heart, just that I would be able to continue to stay on the roster and be with the team the rest of the year," Lin said.

A week later came that desperation game in Boston, when D'Antoni inserted Lin into the game because he felt almost out of other options. The day after that was February 4, with the Knicks playing the Nets at Madison Square Garden. And that, finally, was Lin's NBA opportunity, his 25-point breakout game. It was a stunning and unexpected performance, of course, but when you consider what Lin had done in the past with opportunities, maybe it shouldn't have been. Lin later reflected on getting his

chance in New York, where he hadn't gotten one with the
Warriors. "I wouldn't say that Golden State wasn't suitable for
me," Lin said. "I think that was—I think I have grown as a player,
and I think in terms of personnel, there is more opportunity here."

Starting with the performance against the Nets, Lin averaged
23.9 points and 9.2 assists in his first 11 games. There are cases in
which players buried deep on the bench immediately succeed
when given a chance, but Lin's numbers were astounding. He was
named the Eastern Conference player of the week, and his 109
points in his first four games in the starting lineup were the most
scored by any player since the NBA-ABA merger in 1976, top-
ping the likes of Shaquille O'Neal and Michael Jordan. Lin also
became the first player to score at least 20 points with seven assists
in each of his first four starts, and he was the youngest player in
league history to average 25 points and eight assists over a five-
game span. However you juggled the numbers, they all pointed to
Lin doing something that the league had never seen in its history.

"Jeremy Lin is a great, great story," Timberwolves All-Star
power forward Kevin Love said. "He's a success story. He has
worked tremendously hard to get where he's at, and he's taken
full advantage of his opportunity. It's going to be a feel-good
story for the NBA, it's good for New York, it's good for the
Knicks. And it's great for the NBA, so you've got to be happy to
see a guy like him do that."

That's been a hallmark of Lin's career, playing well when
opportunity arises. But the opportunity with the Knicks was
much bigger than any he'd had before, bigger than that state
championship game and those AAU tournaments and the BC
game and the summer league matchup with Wall. With that
opportunity, Lin was at his best.

"Great kid and he's a hell of a player," said NBA veteran and TNT analyst Steve Kerr. "It makes you wonder how many guys are out there who have just slipped through the cracks and didn't find the right circumstances. But that's what this league is about for, I think, the majority of players in the league. It's finding the right coach, the right system, the right teammates and even catching some breaks, injury-wise, playing time-wise, and I am sure there are lots of guys who have slipped through the cracks. What I'm most impressed with Jeremy is that when he got his opportunity, he didn't just grab it. He choked it by the neck. He basically just took over the whole franchise, which is stunning, because it is New York and it's Melo and Amar'e. You've got stars, you've got the media capital of the world, and he just seized it and grabbed it and he's not letting go."

Yes, of all the places for Lin to achieve stardom, New York figures prominently in his story. There is no other market in sports that can match the intensity of media scrutiny—combine that with a basketball team that has not won a playoff game in more than a decade and that was off to a poor start this season, and the circumstances for Lin's shooting-star story were just right. "I think obviously playing in New York, it's a big stage with a big fan base, and so there's a lot of media," Lin said. "And I think in terms of platform and media, I think that's the best place to be, New York, just because they have it all."

Having it all, though, can be pleasant when things are going well. But it works both ways.

CHAPTER 4

ADAPT TO SUCCESS

"The journey was very different; it's been tough
at times. My family has been through a lot. All of
us, my whole family, the whole last year-and-half,
the downs we had to go through. But God is
faithful and he put us on this unbelievable journey."

—*Jeremy Lin*

February 24, 2012
Amway Arena
Orlando, Florida

There is a large conference room off the tunnel underneath the stands at the Amway Center in Orlando, encircling the basketball court. It served as the makeshift interview room for this year's All-Star weekend, with a stage up front, under bright lights and in front of rows of dozens of chairs. League MVP candidates like Kevin Durant and LeBron James conducted their press sessions there, as well as this year's likely Rookie of the Year winner, Kyrie Irving. It was also the site of the jam-packed annual press conference held by NBA commissioner David Stern and deputy commissioner Adam Silver, for which media members had to stand in the aisles.

But the most unusual interviewee in the room that weekend was Knicks point guard Jeremy Lin, who was participating in the BBVA Rising Stars challenge, a minor game matching a mix of rookies against second-year players. Those players would usually be available to a small group of media on the morning before the game, but because Lin had garnered so much attention in the previous weeks, the league decided he would require special arrangements, and a pregame press conference was put together.

It was packed, with at least as many members of the media—if not more—as had been at Stern's session.

Lin was the talk of All-Star weekend. Originally, he wasn't even supposed to be included, with voting for the players who would participate in the Rising Stars game having concluded before Lin caught fire with the Knicks. At the press conference, he was shocked just to see so many people gathered to talk to him. He was asked about the "Linsanity" phenomenon and whether he had come up with a "Lin"-based pun, as so many New York newspapers had. "I just like 'Jeremy,'" he responded. "I want to make sure I don't change as a person and that I don't let any of this get to me."

And, soon after, he was asked whether he was ready for the hoopla to go away. "I'm definitely surprised that people are still talking about Linsanity or whatever," he said. "I think hopefully as the season progresses, it will go from that to New York Knicks, and hopefully the Knicks can win basketball games, we can make a good push after the All Star Break, and people will start talking about the Knicks and not necessarily me."

———————

For weeks heading into All-Star weekend, though, just about everything seemed to be going Lin's way, and there was no way to avoid Lin chatter. The Knicks were winning, and though they had not beaten the league's elite teams, they were exciting again—Lin made a previously dreary set of players suddenly fun to watch. Having seen them on February 3, in the game before Lin's breakout performance, and having studied them on film since, Celtics coach Doc Rivers said he noticed that the Knicks were finally having fun. "They're playing different," Rivers said. "They're a different team. I think they have a different spirit. They were just kind of going through it when we played them the last time. Now you can see they believe that they're a good basketball team, that they can win basketball games and that they can challenge. When you have that kind of spirit, you become a better team, and they have it."

One week before the All-Star game, Lin and the Knicks had their stiffest test, playing the defending-champion Mavericks on their home floor. One of Lin's fellow Knicks, Tyson Chandler, had played with Dallas the previous season and spent some time with his old teammates before the game. They were prepared for Lin, they told Chandler, and their defense would be ready.

But Lin sliced through the Mavericks' defense, scoring 28 points and dishing out 14 assists. The Knicks won, 104-97, maybe their most impressive victory of the season. Over and over again, the Knicks hit Dallas with pick-and-rolls, a staple play for many NBA offenses. The pick-and-roll can be set up quickly, forces the defense to shuffle players into mismatches, and provides the point guard with numerous options. Generally, a center—in the Knicks' case, Amar'e Stoudemire or Chandler—will step out about 20 feet from the basket, bringing his defender, usually another big man, with him. The point guard will dribble toward his teammate, who will "pick" the point guard's defender. That means the defense must decide whether to switch defensive assignments (leaving an undersize point guard on the big man and a slow-footed big man on the point guard) or to work around the pick, which leaves the point guard with some space to either drive to the basket, make a pass, or shoot.

"Oh, it is by far the most important play in our game," Hall of Fame coach and ABC analyst Hubie Brown said. "Every coach, no matter what you run or however many pages you've got in the playbook, you're going to have a big percentage of your plays that are pick-and-roll plays or some variation on it. It depends how well you run it, but for every coach, it is like bread and butter."

The play was especially important in D'Antoni's offense. Back in D'Antoni's first full season as a coach in the NBA, in Phoenix in 2004–05, he helped lead an offensive revolution around the league, coaching a team that emphasized speed, fast-break play, and pick-and-rolls—that Suns team's motto was "seven seconds or less," meaning they tried to get a shot up within seven seconds of gaining possession of the ball. If they could not score quickly, they usually would go right into pick-and-roll action. Those Suns (which included a younger Stoudemire, who left Phoenix to join D'Antoni in New York in 2010) averaged 110.4 points per game, a scoring mark that had not been reached in 10 years in what had become an increasingly defensive-minded NBA. The Suns won the most games in the league (62), ranked second in fast-break points per game, and were No. 1 in points coming off pick-and-roll plays. The team's point guard, Steve Nash, went on to win the MVP award, the first of two in a row, and led the NBA in assists with 11.5 per game.

Well before he had any idea that he eventually would wind up with the Knicks, Lin worked relentlessly on pick-and-roll performance at Reno of the D League. Coach Eric Musselman said that Lin wanted to learn to see the whole floor, to be able to keep all of his teammates involved. If a point guard running pick-and-rolls becomes too focused on himself and the man who is setting the pick, the play becomes easy to defend. "Jeremy said he wanted to be able to come off the pick and make passes to shoot-ers, rather than making things into a strictly two-man game," Musselman said. "The goal was to get him to use a true five-man offense, to make everyone a threat, especially the 3-point shoot-ers on the other side of the floor. He worked hard at it. You could see him really improve as he went."

In D'Antoni's offense, that hard work would pay off. Lin thrived in the pick-and-roll, especially when the Knicks were able to space out the floor with outside shooters like Steve Novak (who had been Lin's teammate at Reno for one game) and the newly acquired guard, J. R. Smith. It was Mavericks general manager Donnie Nelson who first made the comparison of Lin to Steve Nash, back on draft night 2010, but the more Lin played in D'Antoni's system, the more others made the compar-ison, too. After the Dallas game, 18-year veteran Jason Kidd, a former teammate of Nash, said, "He is looking a little bit like Steve Nash out there."

Hall of Fame point guard Earvin "Magic" Johnson, arguably the greatest ever to play the position, agreed, finding similarities in the way Nash and Lin used start-and-stop motion—more than speed, size, and agility—to throw defenders off balance. "He plays like Steve Nash," Johnson said. "He comes off the pick not looking to blow past you, he comes off the pick to make you stop. Because he stops. He has a great stop-and-go move, and he is always surveying the floor. It's not about him. So he reads the defense. You fall back, he will take the little jumper. You come up, he will try to get around you to pass it to an open man. This guy is for real. For real. He's smart enough, and he is clever enough."

Lin himself knew that there was something special about the way he meshed with D'Antoni's offense, and that he was lucky to be in that system. There were some observers who scoffed that Lin was successful only because of the system. But Lin embraced that notion. "I think pick-and-roll-wise, that's always been something, looking back even in high school, we ran a lot of pick-and-rolls, and in college we ran a lot of pick-and-rolls, so that's just something that's kind of developed over time, just being familiar with pick-and-rolls," he said. "I know there's the theory that it's just a perfect system for me, and so, I agree it is a perfect system for me, and I'm thankful that I play for Coach D'Antoni."

In the NBA, or in any major professional sport, things can change quickly, no matter how perfect. Every coach sees offense differently—where some prefer to run plays that keep all options open, other prefer to hammer the ball to the team's best players and allow them to make plays on their own, with the rest of the team acting as a supporting cast.

——————— ▬▬▬▬▬▬ ———————

While things were perfect, while the Knicks were playing with that renewed spirit, while the team was winning and Lin's star was at its peak, one of the most impressive aspects of the Lin story was the way he handled the crush of attention—calmly, with careful calculation and a consistent deflection of credit to those around him. Lin remained collected, no matter how outlandish things got. When he was in college, Lin has said, he faced pretty consistent and sophomoric taunts from opposing fans about his ethnicity. Lin's emergence spawned everything from puns in poor taste to patently racist commentary in the mainstream media and on social media. But he took it in stride, even when an ESPN website editor (and, separately, a radio personality for the network) used the phrase, "A Chink in the Armor," as a headline after the Knicks' first loss with Lin as a starter. The network quickly apologized, firing the headline writer and suspending the radio host. Lin shrugged off any controversy by saying he accepted the apology and hoped to move on quickly.

Players around the league, even star players, took notice. "He's a tough-minded guy to go through what he's gone through, to be cut twice in one year and come back and perform at the level he's performed at," Heat guard Dwyane Wade told reporters. "Someone like that, you just want to see them be who they are and not change no matter what. Because in this league, there's going to be a lot of highs and there's going to be a lot of lows. You have to stay even-keeled as much as possible. He seems like he is a level-headed guy and he can deal with it."

But while Lin is level-headed, he also has shown the kind of characteristics, even during those light-speed Linsanity weeks, that would indicate a willingness to continue recognizing his faults and addressing them. First on the list is that Lin maintained his humility throughout the entire whirlwind experience. "He's extremely humble," teammate Landry Fields said. "That has not changed. He is handling everything very well, and at the end of the day, he's only human. We're going to have off games, because it is the NBA. But with his character and the kind of player he is, he is going to bounce back strong. He has done that over and over. He doesn't take bad things—nine turnovers, a bad shooting day, whatever it may be—and dwell on it. He is going to go right back out there and keep doing what he does."

There was no doubt, too, that Lin was connecting with the denizens of Madison Square Garden, a sometimes tough crowd.

The speed with which New York fans embraced Lin was remarkable, and showed how much Knicks fans—who have been disappointed by star acquisitions Carmelo Anthony and Stoudemire over the last two years—have been searching for a player worth rooting for.

"He's playing great basketball, and New Yorkers love it when people are playing great for their city, or just playing hard," teammate Bill Walker said. "They definitely embrace him. I am happy for him. He deserves it a lot. You can tell that he just works extremely hard at his game to get where he is today. He's not even like all of the [Linsanity]. He's just so humble and he doesn't care about outside stuff. He's just playing basketball. Of course, I'm pretty sure he's happy when he's playing well, when he's getting all this attention, but he's a humble dude."

A humble dude who has remained true to his faith, in good fortune and when faced with challenges. That's an important aspect of Lin's character. There was a time, while at Harvard, that Lin was considering becoming a youth minister—before he decided to give the NBA a shot. Lin doesn't use his fame to proselytize, but he has not been shy about crediting God with his success. He regularly sends out Bible verses to his Twitter followers, and in mid-March, when a Twitter follower sent a tweet to him with only the word, "Chink," in it, Lin responded: "This is happening in 2012? Jesus loves you bro and I do too."

When he was asked why he chose to wear uniform No. 17 with the Knicks, the assumption was that it was an homage to Chris Mullin, the Hall of Fame forward for the Warriors and one of Lin's favorite players as a kid growing up in the Bay Area. But Lin said, "Seven was my number last year, and it's one of God's numbers that he uses throughout the Bible. And I chose

17 because the '1' was supposed to, kind of, to represent me and the '7' was to represent God. And for me, when I went to the D League, I had 17, so everywhere I go, He would be right there next to me. So that's why I stuck with 17."

There is his family, too, which has supported him throughout his pursuit of his basketball career. Lin is very close with his parents and with his two brothers. His older brother, Josh, is the NYU dental student whose couch Lin called his bed when he first arrived in New York to play for the Knicks on his nonguaranteed deal, and his younger brother, Joseph, is a freshman basketball player at Div. III Hamilton College in Clinton, NY. Lin's father, Gie-Ming, is known to be a basketball junkie who would play with his sons regularly at the YMCA in Palo Alto. In a December 2009 article in *Time* magazine, Gie-Ming said, "Many Asian families focus so much on academics. But it felt so good to play with my kids. I enjoyed it so much."

Lin's family was instrumental in getting him through the trips to the D League, the lack of playing time, and the uncertainty about his career. They'll be instrumental in getting him through his next set of hurdles, too. "We're just thankful," Lin said. "The journey was very different, it's been tough at times. My family has been through a lot. All of us, my whole family, the whole last year and a half, the downs we had to go through. But God is faithful and he put us on this unbelievable journey. We're just trying to enjoy everything right now and we're trying to stay together and make sure that we handle everything the right way. That's what we're focused on."

CHAPTER 5

GROW FROM ADVERSITY

"When you become a good player, the scouting report starts to figure you out. That's something that Carmelo and I faced our whole careers. So that's something that he's going to have to get used to, but we are gonna help him out."

—*Amar'e Stoudemire*

March 12, 2012
United Center
Chicago, Illinois

With 4:37 to play in the second quarter of a Monday night game against the Bulls, Jeremy Lin was lining up to play defense against Bulls guard Derrick Rose, the league's reigning MVP and the No. 1 draft pick in the NBA's 2008 draft. As talented as he is—there isn't a point guard in the league who matches Rose for his combination of speed and strength—Rose is generally mild-mannered on the court. But he seemed especially animated on this night.

Rose took an outlet pass from teammate Taj Gibson about 70 feet from the basket and quickly surveyed the floor. He got to the top of the 3-point line and made a jab step to the left, throwing Lin off his balance before Rose bolted hard to the right. Lin tried to recover, but Rose scooped up the ball in his right arm, the way an NFL running back cradles a football, put his shoulder into Lin's chest and drove to the basket. Knicks center Josh Harrellson came over, attempting to provide help on defense, but Rose finished the layup for a basket.

After Lin responded by throwing a crafty deep pass to Carmelo Anthony for a fast-break basket, Rose just looked annoyed—he again drove down and set Lin up at the top of the 3-point line, this time leaning into Lin as he took a 16-foot jumper to draw a foul, against Lin's protestations. On the Bulls' next possession, Rose again attacked Lin, and gave the referee a brief look of disgust when he failed to call a reach-in foul. Rose shook off the noncall, sized up Lin again, and blew past him to the left, beating Lin to the hoop by two strides and again finishing a layup off the backboard.

Rose finished with 32 points and seven assists, attempting 29 shots. Lin played well, with 15 points and eight assists, but he was no match for Rose. The Bulls won, 104-99, giving the Knicks their sixth straight loss. After the game, Rose was asked whether he had played with added aggressiveness, because of hype that had arisen around Lin. "Definitely," Rose responded. "Who's not right now?"

In the visiting locker room, meanwhile, frustration was simmering. Anthony told reporters, "It sucks. The situation we're in right now sucks. Losing basketball games the way we have been at the end of games sucks. It's not a good feeling."

For Lin, this was bound to happen. The peak of Lin's rise came during the team's string of eight wins in nine games in February, a run that pulled Knicks back to .500. But things began changing after that, and disillusionment set in after the Knicks turned around and lost eight of 10 games. The problem started, simply enough, with familiarity. When a player rises to prominence as quickly as Lin did, one of the problems for opponents is that there simply has not been time to scout him. Most players in the league have seen each other plenty of times, over the course of years playing against each other in the NBA and in the off-season. But a new guy like Lin has the element of surprise on his side. Defenders don't know his tendencies, don't know what kind of shots he likes to take, don't know where his weaknesses are and how to take advantage of them. It takes time and careful study of game films to figure those things out.

It is the kind of pattern that teammate Amar'e Stoudemire had gone through himself, back when he was a raw rookie sensation in Phoenix in 2002. Stoudemire made a big initial impression, but over that season, his tendencies became easier to read, and his inability to handle the ball and shoot midrange jumpers gave teams a blueprint to defend him—which, in turn, gave Stoudemire a clear understanding of what he needed to work on. "When you become a good player, the scouting report starts to figure you out," Stoudemire said. "That's something that Carmelo and I faced our whole careers. So that's something that he's going to have to get used to, but we are gonna help him out."

Even as he had been leading the Knicks to wins, Lin had shown a particular penchant to force the ball into bad spots, causing turnovers. The Knicks could withstand that, though, especially because Lin made so many outstanding, albeit risky, plays to go along with those turnovers. There was confidence, too, that Lin would learn from experience and reduce his turnovers as he went on. Generally, four turnovers in a game by a point guard is considered too many, but in his first start, Lin committed eight turnovers. He then had four or more in 12 of his first 17 games as a starter, and that became part of the scouting report on Lin: Be physical with him and it will lead to turnovers. Scouts also figured out that Lin almost exclusively prefers to go to his right, and that, despite his marked shooting improvements, he still is not nearly as much of a scoring threat with his jumper as he is driving to the basket.

Lin was not just been the target of scouting reports and film sessions, though. He has also become the target of opponents' egos—having racked up so much attention, players now take pride in focusing their defense on him and attacking him offensively, as Derrick Rose admitted he had done. Other opposing point guards seemed to take the matchup personally, too. None more so than Boston's Rajon Rondo, who had one of the best games of the year for any point guard, or any player for that matter, notching 18 points, 17 rebounds and 20 assists against Lin, prompting Celtics teammate Kevin Garnett to say, "The thing about Lin is I think everybody who's at the point guard position is going to be excited to play the kid. [Rondo] was nothing short of that today. I could see it."

There were more, too. New Jersey's Deron Williams scored 38 points in a win over New York. The Spurs' Tony Parker posted 32 points against the Knicks. "Now, he has to know guys are going to be gunning for him," Sixers All-Star Andre Iguodala said. "When you make a name for yourself like that, you are going to be tested, and that's what is going to happen to him now. And he has to play in a tough place, he is definitely under the microscope in New York City. He got thrown into the fire right away, though, and he handled it, so it will be interesting to see how he handles it now that he has all the attention and the accolades."

But it wasn't just scouts, coaches, and opposing players that conspired to slow Lin and the Knicks—no, there was also a major problem with personnel on his own team. D'Antoni's system works best when there is an athletic big man, like Chandler or a healthy Stoudemire, to set the pick, and when there are plenty of good outside shooters stationed on the 3-point line to spread the floor. The Knicks have that arrangement only sometimes. First, there was the challenge of working Stoudemire back into the lineup, which was not easy because Stoudemire had been dealing with injuries and appeared a step slower all season. Stoudemire averaged 25.3 points in 2010–11, and, since he was a rookie, has averaged more than 20 points every year he's been healthy. During the 2011–12 season, his scoring average is below 18 points.

Still, Stoudemire was, at least, a believer in the Knicks' share-the-shots offense, even if it meant a lesser role for him. But Carmelo Anthony, a five-time All-Star whose career scoring average is nearly 25 points per game, had missed the bulk of the Linsanity run with a groin injury. His return to the Knicks lineup just as the pick-and-roll was turning into such a devastating weapon was cause for concern, because he is a ball-dominating forward who is not really a pick-and-roll player. Anthony is not content to stand behind the 3-point line and wait for the ball to swing to him the way a role player like Steve Novak is— throughout his career in the NBA, and going back to his collegiate days at Syracuse, Anthony has always had the offense run through him, not through the point guard. And he has never been much of a long-distance shooter.

Back in February 2011, when the Knicks traded four of their top six players to Denver for Anthony and Chauncey Billups, many questioned whether Anthony would be the kind of player who could ever fit with D'Antoni's system. Rob Mahoney, in the *New York Times*'s Off-the-Dribble blog, wrote, "The acquisitions of Anthony and Billups are hardly a perfect marriage between personnel and scheme, but the obvious hope in New York is that talent wins out. There's no question that Anthony and Billups both can be tremendously effective offensive players, but the uncertainty in this deal stems from whether their individual success can coincide with the successful execution of the Knicks' offense."

Turns out there was good cause for that uncertainty. Before Anthony and Stoudemire returned from injuries, when the Knicks were in Toronto, Lin acknowledged that some things would have to be different in the days ahead. The Knicks' early success with Lin at the helm was aided by some weak foes, but the team was also succeeding because it was able to run an unadulterated version of D'Antoni's offense, something the Knicks couldn't do with their previous point guards or with Anthony as the focal point. "I am just part of the team," Lin said. "I think that's the most important thing, we're all trying to find where we can fit in and what we can do to help the team win, where our role is. Obviously that is going to change a little going forward with two of the Top 10 scorers in the league coming back."

———————————

Two days after the loss to the Bulls, the Knicks held their normal morning shootaround at their facility in Greenburgh, NY, ahead of their game with Portland that night. But there was discontent in the air. A report in the *New York Post* that morning cited a source close to Anthony describing the unhappiness of the Knicks star and claimed that Anthony wanted to be traded. Anthony denied that report, and at the shootaround, he said he was "100 percent" behind D'Antoni. For his part, D'Antoni was reportedly upbeat that morning. But he'd also decided that there was no way he could allow the Knicks' season to continue on its current path.

D'Antoni met with team officials and told them it might be in the best interests of the team if he stepped aside. According to multiple reports, he floated the idea of trading Anthony to team owner James Dolan, but Dolan—who was instrumental in orchestrating the trade for Anthony in the first place, despite D'Antoni's objections—rejected the idea. So D'Antoni walked away, seeing that there would be no resolution between the style of play he wanted to see and the style that having Anthony on the roster requires, and he was afraid that the clash would lead to the Knicks missing the playoffs. D'Antoni left the team to assistant Mike Woodson, a veteran coach who had run the Hawks, on an interim basis.

For Lin, it was a devastating blow. There were coaches who had believed in Lin and had boosted him along his career path, but D'Antoni had shown the ultimate faith—he had made Lin a starter in the NBA, and put him in a system that showed the talents Lin had. Even as Lin had made mistakes, D'Antoni kept up his faith in him. "Obviously, I miss him a lot," Lin told reporters after the Knicks' first game under Woodson. "What he did for my career, I am not going to forget what he did for me personally. It was very emotional. I'm sad to see him go. I owe a lot to him."

Tommy Amaker, Lin's coach at Harvard, heard the news about D'Antoni's departure as the Crimson were about to play their first NCAA tournament game in 66 years, against Vanderbilt in Albuquerque, New Mexico. "I just thought that the style and the system was ideally suited for him," Amaker said. "I thought that's what allowed him to blossom as well as he did and as early as he did.... Obviously, that could be a tough blow—not only for Jeremy but their team and their organization."

Lin joked that, having been through three NBA teams and two D League teams in the past year, finding his way in a new offensive system is nothing he hasn't done before. He could make the adjustments needed to play the way Woodson wants. But once again, Lin will have to adapt to adversity, because Woodson's offense is much heavier on the kind of post-ups and isolation plays that Anthony favors—not the pick-and-rolls that earned Lin so many comparisons to Steve Nash. One of the reasons Woodson was replaced when he was coaching in Atlanta was that management felt his offense was too reliant on simply putting the ball in the hands of star player Joe Johnson on isolation plays, and not involving other players enough.

The style of play that sparked Linsanity in the first place is on the wane in New York, and Lin's role on the team is, thus, in flux. But Lin has said all along that he is prepared for this sort of thing. As many things as his flight of stardom was—fun, stunning, inspiring, brief—Lin has never fooled himself into thinking that he had reached his goal or was at the end of his journey. Lin's story is just beginning, and as he has shown, no matter what the obstacles, no matter what the weaknesses in his game, no matter how focused opposing defenses are on him, he will find ways to grow from adversity.

"I understood that I had a lot of growth as a player and I have a lot right now," Lin said. "I have been able to get away with some stuff, but defenses are going to start locking in, and so I am going to have to improve, and I know that. And so it's a continual process."

EPILOGUE

"I am just trying to take it all in and embrace it."

—*Jeremy Lin*

There are those who are just well equipped to handle adversity and come through with toughness, and there are those who have taught themselves toughness through experience. Dr. Jason Selk, a motivational speaker and author who also was the Director of Mental Toughness for the St. Louis Cardinals, has spent a lot of time on the subject. As Selk sees it, most people approach adversity by using Problem-Centric Thought (PCT), which is to say they see a problem and focus on the negatives that come along with that problem. But some people are predisposed, by some combination of genetics and environment, to approach problems with what Selk calls a Relentless Solution Focus (RSF)—they see problems and simply begin working on solutions.

You might have a car accident and fall into a funk worrying about the bills that will come with fixing the damage and the problems with getting to work. Or you might immediately come up with a way to donate your car for a tax deduction and resolve to ride your bike more. "You can train yourself to look at things through the RSF lens rather than the PCT lens," Selk said. "But there are people who just naturally approach life with the RSF outlook. They don't get burdened by problems, they almost get excited about working on ways to fix the problems. That's something that, with athletes, is almost a natural transition that you have to make, because you're going to face adversity in every game, and certainly working within the confines of your team."

There is probably adversity ahead for Jeremy Lin, but there's also plenty of reason to believe that he will somehow come up with solutions. He's tried to stay positive over the last two years (and beyond), no matter how many twists his basketball life has taken. When Lin was asked what his backup plans were had he been cut by the Knicks in January, which was a very real possibility, he said, "I really didn't have a plan B, to be honest. I wasn't sure. Obviously I was thinking about three main options: overseas, D League, or to just take a break or give up basketball for a while. And I just didn't really know. I was just trying not to think about it, basically So I just said, if I get cut by the Knicks, then I will take a look at all of that, but until that happens, I want to make sure I try to stay focused and not think negatively."

He has been through it before, after all, having gone unrecruited by most colleges, having gone undrafted by the NBA, having made those trips to the developmental league, having been waived twice. Lin's past responses to those situations—addressing his problems with shooting lessons, tightening his body with his work at the Sparta facility in the off-season, his approach to his demotions to the D League as a chance to improve on his game—suggest Selk's RSF mindset, a certain amount of toughness. Some of that is probably inborn. He did grow up with two parents who stressed academics, and he did graduate from Harvard with a 3.1 GPA. That requires a pretty relentless focus on solutions.

How and where those solutions are employed will be a sideshow that the entire NBA will be watching. There's no question that the league is a political machine, that there is always more at stake than meets the eye when it comes to the inner workings of a team, whether it is how minutes on the floor and shot attempts are distributed, how trades are worked out, or which coaches stay and which coaches leave. For the Knicks, Carmelo Anthony is slated to make $18.5 million this year, the eighth-highest paycheck in the league, and will earn $19.5 million next season. Lin was to earn $788,000 this year and is unsigned for next season. Anthony has the most powerful group of agents in the NBA—Creative Artists Agency, which also represents LeBron James, Dwyane Wade, and Chris Paul—behind him. Lin has Roger Montgomery, a hard-working but small-scale agent whose only other current NBA client is veteran reserve Maurice Evans.

If there is to be a tug-of-war over which style wins out, Anthony's style or the pick-and-roll play that most Knicks seemed to favor and that benefited Lin so dramatically, then there should be no surprise that Knicks ownership voted for Anthony. That's normal NBA politics. There should be no surprise, too, that Mike Woodson, in his first practice running the team, recalled his early days as a rookie Knicks player in 1980. "I remember playing for a great coach in Red Holzman," Woodson said. "He taught me rookies were to sit, listen, and learn. He taught me a valuable lesson way back when. I listened and learned a lot as a rookie."

Lin is not a rookie, of course, but Woodson's message is clear—Lin should not complain, should be quiet, and should focus on learning. Sure that February stretch in which Lin dominated was nice, sure it might very well have saved the team's season, and sure it was probably the most exciting time for the franchise in a decade. But now the Knicks seemed to be saying that they wanted to leave the winning to the grown-ups.

Lin himself probably will have to repeat the very lessons that were evident in the story of his remarkable rise. He will, again, have to pull his career along its very odd trajectory and get comfortable on the road less traveled. He will, again, have to work hard to improve on his natural talent. He will, again, have to find a coach and an organization willing to give him the opportunity that D'Antoni and (for a while) the Knicks gave him, and he will again have to seize that opportunity. It's likely, too, that Lin will, again, have to adapt to successes and grow from failures. He's already done these things once, of course.

All of this might not happen in New York. The Knicks, in the coming weeks and months, will have plenty of questions to answer—Can they hire former Knick Phil Jackson as coach? Can Stoudemire return to full health? Does their core of players have enough talent to really be a champion?—but one of the chief questions figures to be what to do with Lin, a free agent who, if only for a short while, was the biggest star in basketball and brought such joy to Madison Square Garden.

If he never quite reaches that level again, if he is never again the most famous sports celebrity in the world, as he seemed to be for a while there, then there is probably one last lesson that can be learned from Lin's strange, strange journey—enjoy every day of it. Time and time again, that has been Lin's message. "I am just trying to take it all in and embrace it," Lin said. "Enjoy it every step of the way."

APPENDIX

STATISTICS

College Career

Year	Team	GP	MIN	PPG	RPG	APG	SPG	BPG	TPG	FG%	FT%	3P%
2006–07	Harvard Crimson	28	18.1	4.8	2.5	1.8	1.0	0.1	1.8	42%	82%	28%
2007–08	Harvard Crimson	30	31.3	12.6	4.8	3.6	1.9	0.6	2.8	45%	62%	28%
2008–09	Harvard Crimson	28	34.8	17.8	5.5	4.3	2.4	0.6	3.8	50%	74%	40%
2009–10	Harvard Crimson	29	32.2	16.4	4.4	4.4	2.4	1.1	3.1	52%	76%	34%

Professional Rookie Season

Year	Team	GP	MIN	PPG	RPG	APG	SPG	BPG	TPG	FG%	FT%	3P%
2010–11	Golden State Warriors	29	9.8	2.6	1.2	1.4	1.1	0.3	0.6	39%	76%	20%

"Linsanity" Game-by-Game (Through Coach Mike D'antoni's Resignation)

Date	Opponent	Result	MIN	Points	Rebounds	Assists	Steals	Blocks	Turn Overs	FG%	FT%	3P%
2/3/12	@ Boston Celtics	L: 89–91	7	2	2	1	0	0	1	0%	100%	0%
2/4/12	New Jersey Nets	W: 99–92	36	25	5	7	3	2	1	53%	71%	0%
2/6/12	Utah Jazz	W: 99–88	45	28	2	8	2	0	8	59%	78%	33%
2/8/12	@ Washington Wizards	W: 107–93	36	23	4	10	2	1	2	64%	83%	0%

(continued on next page)

Date	Opponent	Result	MIN	Points	Rebounds	Assists	Steals	Blocks	Turn Overs	FG%	FT%	3P%
2/10/12	Los Angeles Lakers	W:92–85	39	38	4	7	2	0	6	57%	77%	50%
2/11/12	@Minnesota Timberwolves	W:100–98	39	20	6	8	3	0	6	33%	57%	0%
2/14/12	@Toronto Raptors	W:90–87	43	27	2	11	1	0	8	45%	64%	100%
2/15/12	Sacramento Kings	W:100–85	26	10	5	13	0	0	6	67%	67%	0%
2/17/12	New Orleans Hornets	L:85–89	40	26	2	5	4	0	9	44%	80%	40%
2/19/12	Dallas Mavericks	W:104–97	46	28	4	14	5	1	7	55%	50%	50%
2/20/12	New Jersey Nets	L:92–100	36	21	7	9	4	0	3	39%	83%	50%
2/22/12	Atlanta Hawks	W:99–82	32	17	2	9	2	0	4	55%	100%	50%
2/23/12	@Miami Heat	L:88–102	34	8	6	3	3	0	8	9%	100%	0%
2/29/12	Cleveland Cavaliers	W:120–103	33	19	5	13	1	0	1	50%	78%	0%
3/4/12	@Boston Celtics	L:111–115	32	14	4	5	1	0	6	38%	50%	50%
3/6/12	@Dallas Mavericks	L:85–95	33	14	3	7	2	0	2	31%	63%	20%

3/7/12	@ San Antonio Spurs	L: 105-118	30	20	3	4	3	0	1	47%	80%	50%
3/9/12	@ Milwaukee Bucks	L: 114-119	41	20	1	13	4	0	5	57%	60%	50%
3/11/12	Philadelphia 76ers	L: 94-106	37	14	3	7	2	0	6	28%	80%	0%
3/12/12	@ Chicago Bulls	L: 94-104	33	15	1	8	3	3	3	36%	100%	100%

GP   Games Played

MIN   Minutes

PPG   Points Per Game

RPG   Rebounds Per Game

APG   Assists Per Game

SPG   Steals Per Game

BPG   Blocks Per Game

TPG   Turnovers Per Game

FG%   Field Goal Percentage

FT%   Free Throw Percentage

3P%   3-Point Percentage

ABOUT THE AUTHOR

Sean Deveney has been with *The Sporting News* since 1999, covering all major sports, with a focus on pro basketball. Deveney has covered dozens of major championships: the NBA Finals, the World Series, the Super Bowl, the NCAA Tournament, college football's championship game, and the PGA championship. He has written about icons, such as Michael Jordan and Tiger Woods, and less-than-iconic topics including Roger Clemens and the inside world of sports agents. He has been the *Sporting News'* basketball insider for more than a decade and has covered every NBA Finals since 2000.

After graduation from Northwestern University in 1997, Deveney worked as the sports editor for *The Sentry-News* in Slidell, LA, where he won a Louisiana Press Association award for best feature story. A native of Lynn, Mass., who grew up with a passion for the Red Sox and had a limited talent as a second baseman, Deveney also has been honored in *The Best American Sports Writing* anthology for a story about Pedro Martinez. He has been a regular guest on radio programs across the country and has appeared on ESPN, Fox News, CNN, CBS, MSNBC, and Comcast Sports. He is the author of *The Original Curse: Did the Cubs Throw the 1918 World Series to Babe Ruth's Red Sox and Incite the Black Sox Scandal?*

The Leadership Legacy of John Wooden:
Inspiration and Lessons You Can Apply Every Day.

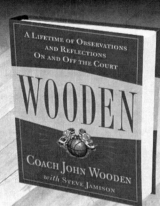

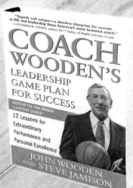

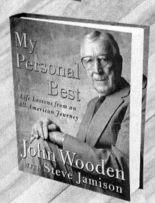

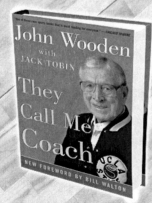

CPSIA information can be obtained at www.ICGtesting.com
Printed in the USA
LVOW111413220312

274321LV00001B/4/P

9 780071 803991